contents

BARS, BROWNIES & TREATS

19

24

42

55

classic favorites

Peanut Butter Glazed Chocolate Bars

¾	cup (1½ sticks) butter or margarine
½	cup HERSHEY'S® Cocoa
1½	cups sugar
1½	teaspoons vanilla extract
3	eggs
1¼	cups all-purpose flour
¼	teaspoon baking powder
	PEANUT BUTTER FILLING AND GLAZE (recipe follows)
	CHOCOLATE DRIZZLE (recipe follows)

1 Heat oven to 350°F. Line 15½ × 10½ × 1-inch jelly-roll pan with foil; grease foil.

2 Melt butter in medium saucepan over low heat. Add cocoa; stir constantly until smooth. Remove from heat; stir in sugar and vanilla. Beat in eggs, one at a time, until well combined. Stir in flour and baking powder. Spread batter evenly in prepared pan.

3 Bake 14 to 16 minutes or until top springs back when touched lightly in center. Remove from oven; cool 2 minutes. Invert onto wire rack. Peel off foil; turn right side up on wire rack to cool completely.

4 Prepare PEANUT BUTTER FILLING AND GLAZE. Cut brownie in half; spread half of glaze evenly on one half. Top with second half; spread with remaining glaze. Cool until glaze is set. Prepare CHOCOLATE DRIZZLE; drizzle over glaze. After chocolate is set, cut into bars.

Peanut Butter Filling and Glaze:

Combine ⅓ cup sugar and ⅓ cup water in small saucepan; cook over medium heat to boiling. Remove from heat; immediately add 1⅔ cups (10-ounce package) REESE'S® Peanut Butter Chips. Stir until melted. Cool slightly. Makes about 1⅓ cups glaze.

Chocolate Drizzle:
Place ⅓ cup HERSHEY'S® SPECIAL DARK Chocolate Chips or HERSHEY'S® Semi-Sweet Chocolate Chips and 1 teaspoon shortening (do not use butter, margarine, spread or oil) in small microwave-safe bowl. Microwave at MEDIUM (50%) 30 seconds to 1 minute or until chips are melted and mixture is smooth when stirred.

Chip and Nut Blondie Cake Bars

MAKES ABOUT 24 BARS

½ cup (1 stick) butter or margarine, softened

½ cup sucralose-brown sugar blend

1 egg

1 tablespoon milk

2 teaspoons vanilla extract

1 cup all-purpose flour

½ teaspoon baking soda

¼ teaspoon salt

1⅓ cups (8-ounce package) HERSHEY'S® Sugar Free Chocolate Chips, divided

½ cup coarsely chopped nuts

¼ teaspoon shortening (do not use butter, margarine, spreads or oil)

1 Heat oven to 350°F. Grease 8- or 9-inch square baking pan.

2 Beat butter and brown sugar blend in large bowl until well blended. Add egg, milk and vanilla; beat well. Stir together flour, baking soda and salt; add to butter mixture, beating until well blended.

3 Set aside 2 tablespoons chocolate chips. Stir the remaining chips and nuts into batter. Spread batter in prepared pan.

4 Bake 15 to 20 minutes or until cake begins to pull from sides of pan, toothpick inserted in center comes out clean and surface is lightly browned. (Do not overbake.) Cool completely in pan on wire rack. (As it cools the center will look underbaked.)

5 Place reserved 2 tablespoons chips and shortening in small microwave-safe bowl. Microwave at MEDIUM (50%) 30 seconds; stir. If necessary, microwave at MEDIUM an additional 10 seconds at a time, stirring after each heating, until chips are melted and smooth when stirred. Drizzle melted chocolate over surface of cake; allow to set. Cut into bars.

Chunky Macadamia Bars

MAKES 24 TO 36 BARS

- ¾ cup (1½ sticks) butter or margarine, softened
- 1 cup packed light brown sugar
- ½ cup granulated sugar
- 1 egg
- 1 teaspoon vanilla extract
- 2¼ cups all-purpose flour
- 1 teaspoon baking soda
- 1¾ cups (10-ounce package) HERSHEY'S® MINI KISSES®BRAND Milk Chocolates, divided
- ¾ cup MAUNA LOA® Macadamia Baking Pieces
- VANILLA GLAZE (recipe follows)

1 Heat oven to 375°F.

2 Beat butter, brown sugar and granulated sugar in large bowl until fluffy. Add egg and vanilla; beat well. Add flour and baking soda; blend well. Stir in 1 cup chocolate pieces and nuts; press into ungreased 13×9×2-inch baking pan. Sprinkle with remaining ¾ cup chocolates.

3 Bake 22 to 25 minutes or until golden brown. Cool completely in pan on wire rack. Drizzle VANILLA GLAZE over top; allow to set. Cut into bars.

Vanilla Glaze: Combine 1 cup powdered sugar, 2 tablespoons milk and ½ teaspoon vanilla extract in small bowl; stir until smooth. Makes ⅓ cup glaze.

Double Peanut Butter Paisley Brownies

MAKES ABOUT 24 TO 36 BROWNIES

½   cup (1 stick) butter or margarine, softened

¼   cup REESE'S® Creamy Peanut Butter

1   cup granulated sugar

1   cup packed light brown sugar

3   eggs

1   teaspoon vanilla extract

2   cups all-purpose flour

2   teaspoons baking powder

¼   teaspoon salt

1⅔   cups (10-ounce package) REESE'S® Peanut Butter Chips

½   cup HERSHEY'S® Syrup or HERSHEY'S® SPECIAL DARK® Syrup

1 Heat oven to 350°F. Grease 13×9×2-inch baking pan.

2 Beat butter and peanut butter in large bowl. Add granulated sugar and brown sugar; beat well. Add eggs, one at a time, beating well after each addition. Blend in vanilla.

3 Stir together flour, baking powder and salt; mix into peanut butter mixture, blending well. Stir in peanut butter chips. Spread half of batter in prepared pan; spoon syrup over top. Carefully top with remaining batter; swirl with metal spatula or knife for marbled effect.

4 Bake 40 to 45 minutes or until lightly browned. Cool completely in pan on wire rack. Cut into squares.

Brownies in a Jar

MAKES 1 JAR MIX

1	cup all-purpose flour
½	teaspoon baking powder
¼	teaspoon salt
1½	cups sugar
⅓	cup HERSHEY'S® SPECIAL DARK® Cocoa
1	cup REESE'S® Peanut Butter Chips or HERSHEY'S® Premier White Chips
½	cup HERSHEY'S® Mini Chips Semi-Sweet Chocolate
	BAKING INSTRUCTIONS (recipe follows)

1 Stir together flour, baking powder and salt in a small bowl.

2 Layer the ingredients in a clean 1-quart glass canister or jar in the following order (from bottom to top): sugar, cocoa, flour mixture, peanut butter chips and small chocolate chips. Tap jar gently on the counter to settle each layer before adding the next one. Close jar. Attach card with BAKING INSTRUCTIONS.

BAKING INSTRUCTIONS: Heat oven to 350°F. Grease and flour an 8-inch square baking pan. Combine ½ cup (1 stick) melted and cooled butter and 2 slightly beaten eggs in a large bowl. Gently stir in jar contents. Spread in prepared pan. Bake for 35 minutes. Cool in pan. Cut into bars.

MAKES 16 BROWNIES

Rocky Road Tasty Team Treats

MAKES ABOUT 36 BARS

1½	cups finely crushed thin pretzels or pretzel sticks
¾	cup (1½ sticks) butter or margarine, melted
1	can (14 ounces) sweetened condensed milk (not evaporated milk)
1¾	cups (10-ounce package) HERSHEY'S® MINI KISSES®BRAND Milk Chocolates
3	cups miniature marshmallows
1⅓	cups coarsely chopped pecans or pecan pieces

1 Heat oven to 350°F. Grease bottom and sides of 13×9×2-inch baking pan.

2 Combine pretzels and melted butter in small bowl; press evenly onto bottom of prepared pan. Spread sweetened condensed milk evenly over pretzel layer; layer evenly with chocolates, marshmallows and pecans, in order. Press down firmly on pecans.

3 Bake 20 to 25 minutes or until lightly browned. Cool completely in pan on wire rack. Cut into bars.

All American HEATH® Brownies

MAKES 16 BROWNIES

⅓	cup butter or margarine
3	sections (½ ounce each) HERSHEY'S® Unsweetened Chocolate Baking Bar
1	cup sugar
2	eggs
1	teaspoon vanilla extract
1	cup all-purpose flour
½	teaspoon baking powder
¼	teaspoon salt
1⅓	cups (8-ounce package) HEATH® Milk Chocolate Toffee Bits

1 Heat oven to 350°F. Grease bottom of 8-inch square baking pan.

2 Melt butter and chocolate in medium saucepan over low heat, stirring occasionally. Stir in sugar. Add eggs, one at a time, beating after each addition. Stir in vanilla. Combine flour, baking powder and salt; add to chocolate mixture, stirring until well blended. Spread batter in prepared pan.

3 Bake 20 minutes or until brownie begins to pull away from sides of pan. Remove from oven; sprinkle with toffee bits. Cover tightly with foil and cool completely on wire rack. Remove foil; cut into squares.

Best Fudgey Pecan Brownies

MAKES ABOUT 16 BROWNIES

½ cup (1 stick) butter or margarine, melted

1 cup sugar

1 teaspoon vanilla extract

2 eggs

½ cup all-purpose flour

⅓ cup HERSHEY'S® Cocoa

¼ teaspoon baking powder

¼ teaspoon salt

½ cup coarsely chopped pecans

CHOCOLATE PECAN FROSTING (recipe follows)

Pecan halves

1 Heat oven to 350°F. Lightly grease 8- or 9-inch square baking pan.

2 Beat butter, sugar and vanilla with spoon in large bowl. Add eggs; beat well. Stir together flour, cocoa, baking powder and salt; gradually add to egg mixture, beating until well blended. Stir in chopped pecans. Spread in prepared pan.

3 Bake 20 to 25 minutes or until brownies begin to pull away from sides of pan. Meanwhile, prepare CHOCOLATE PECAN FROSTING. Spread warm frosting over warm brownies. Garnish with pecan halves. Cool completely; cut into squares.

Chocolate Pecan Frosting

1⅓ cups powdered sugar

2 tablespoons HERSHEY'S® Cocoa

3 tablespoons butter or margarine

2 tablespoons milk

¼ teaspoon vanilla extract

¼ cup chopped pecans

1 Stir together powdered sugar and cocoa in medium bowl.

2 Heat butter and milk in small saucepan over low heat until butter is melted. Gradually beat into cocoa mixture, beating until smooth. Stir in vanilla and pecans.

MAKES ABOUT 1 CUP FROSTING

Double Chip Brownies

MAKES ABOUT 36 BROWNIES

¾ cup HERSHEY'S® Cocoa

½ teaspoon baking soda

⅔ cup butter or margarine, melted and divided

½ cup boiling water

2 cups sugar

2 eggs

1⅓ cups all-purpose flour

1 teaspoon vanilla extract

¼ teaspoon salt

1 cup HERSHEY'S® Milk Chocolate Chips

1 cup REESE'S® Peanut Butter Chips

1 Heat oven to 350°F. Grease 13×9×2-inch baking pan.

2 Stir together cocoa and baking soda in large bowl; stir in ⅓ cup melted butter. Add boiling water; stir until mixture thickens. Stir in sugar, eggs and remaining ⅓ cup melted butter; stir until smooth. Add flour, vanilla and salt; blend thoroughly. Stir in milk chocolate chips and peanut butter chips. Spread in prepared pan.

3 Bake 35 to 40 minutes or until brownies begin to pull away from sides of pan. Cool completely in pan on wire rack. Cut into squares.

Chocolate Cranberry Bars

MAKES 36 BARS

2	cups vanilla wafer crumbs (about 60 wafers, crushed)
½	cup HERSHEY'S® Cocoa
3	tablespoons sugar
⅔	cup cold butter, cut into pieces
1	can (14 ounces) sweetened condensed milk (not evaporated milk)
1	cup REESE'S® Peanut Butter Chips
1⅓	cups (6-ounce package) sweetened dried cranberries or 1⅓ cups raisins
1	cup coarsely chopped walnuts

1 Heat oven to 350°F.

2 Stir together vanilla wafer crumbs, cocoa and sugar in medium bowl; cut in butter until crumbly. Press mixture evenly on bottom and ½ inch up sides of 13×9×2-inch baking pan. Pour sweetened condensed milk evenly over crumb mixture; sprinkle evenly with peanut butter chips and dried cranberries. Sprinkle nuts on top; press down firmly.

3 Bake 25 to 30 minutes or until lightly browned. Cool completely in pan on wire rack. Cover with foil; let stand several hours before cutting into bars and serving.

English Toffee Bars

MAKES 24 TO 36 BARS

- **2 cups all-purpose flour**
- **1 cup packed light brown sugar**
- **½ cup (1 stick) cold butter**
- **1 cup pecan halves**
- **TOFFEE TOPPING (recipe follows)**
- **1 cup HERSHEY'S® Milk Chocolate Chips**

1 Heat oven to 350°F.

2 Combine flour and brown sugar in large bowl. With pastry blender or fork, cut in butter until fine crumbs form (a few large crumbs may remain). Press mixture onto bottom of ungreased 13×9×2-inch baking pan. Sprinkle pecans over crust. Prepare TOFFEE TOPPING; drizzle evenly over pecans and crust.

3 Bake 20 to 22 minutes or until topping is bubbly and golden; remove from oven. Immediately sprinkle milk chocolate chips evenly over top; press gently onto surface. Cool completely in pan on wire rack. Cut into bars.

Toffee Topping: Combine ⅔ cup butter and ⅓ cup packed light brown sugar in small saucepan; cook over medium heat, stirring constantly, until mixture comes to a boil. Continue boiling, stirring constantly, 30 seconds. Use immediately.

Thick and Fudgey Brownies with HERSHEY'S. MINI KISSES® Milk Chocolates

MAKES 24 BROWNIES

2¼	cups all-purpose flour
⅔	cup HERSHEY'S® Cocoa
1	teaspoon baking powder
1	teaspoon salt
¾	cup (1½ sticks) butter or margarine, melted
2½	cups sugar
2	teaspoons vanilla extract
4	eggs
1¾	cups (10-ounce package) HERSHEY'S® MINI KISSES®BRAND **Milk Chocolates**

1 Heat oven to 350°F (325°F for glass baking dish). Grease 13×9×2-inch baking pan.

2 Stir together flour, cocoa, baking powder and salt. With spoon or whisk, stir together butter, sugar and vanilla in large bowl. Add eggs; stir until well blended. Stir in flour mixture, blending well. Stir in chocolate pieces. Spread batter in prepared pan.

3 Bake 30 to 35 minutes or until brownies begin to pull away from sides of pan. Cool completely in pan on wire rack; cut into 2-inch squares.

MINI KISSES® Blondies

MAKES ABOUT 36 BARS

- ½ cup (1 stick) butter or margarine, softened
- 1⅓ cups packed light brown sugar
- 2 eggs
- 2 teaspoons vanilla extract
- ¼ teaspoon salt
- 2 cups all-purpose flour
- 1½ teaspoons baking powder
- 1¾ cups (10-ounce package) HERSHEY'S® MINI KISSES®BRAND Milk Chocolates
- ½ cup chopped nuts

1 Heat oven to 350°F. Lightly grease 13×9×2-inch baking pan.

2 Beat butter and brown sugar in large bowl until fluffy. Add eggs, vanilla and salt; beat until blended. Add flour and baking powder; beat just until blended. Stir in chocolate pieces. Spread batter in prepared pan. Sprinkle nuts over top.

3 Bake 28 to 30 minutes or until set and golden brown. Cool completely in pan on wire rack. Cut into bars.

Rocky Road Brownies

1¼	cups miniature marshmallows
1	cup HERSHEY'S® SPECIAL DARK® Chocolate Chips or HERSHEY'S® Semi-Sweet Chocolate Chips
½	cup chopped nuts
½	cup (1 stick) butter or margarine
1	cup sugar
2	eggs
1	teaspoon vanilla extract
½	cup all-purpose flour
⅓	cup HERSHEY'S® Cocoa
½	teaspoon baking powder
½	teaspoon salt

1 Heat oven to 350°F. Grease 9-inch square baking pan.

2 Stir together marshmallows, chocolate chips and nuts; set aside. Place butter in large microwave-safe bowl. Microwave at MEDIUM (50%) 1 to 1½ minutes or until melted. Add sugar, eggs and vanilla, beating with spoon until well blended. Add flour, cocoa, baking powder and salt; blend well. Spread batter in prepared pan.

3 Bake 22 minutes. Sprinkle chocolate chip mixture over top. Continue baking 5 minutes or until marshmallows have softened and puffed slightly. Cool completely. With wet knife, cut into squares.

HERSHEY'S® Brownies with Peanut Butter Frosting

MAKES ABOUT 16 BROWNIES

- ½ cup (1 stick) butter or margarine
- 4 sections (½ ounce each) HERSHEY'S® Unsweetened Chocolate Baking Bar, broken into pieces
- 1 cup sugar
- 2 eggs
- 1 teaspoon vanilla extract
- ½ cup all-purpose flour
- ¼ teaspoon baking powder
- ¼ teaspoon salt
- ½ cup chopped nuts
- PEANUT BUTTER FROSTING (recipe follows, optional)

1 Heat oven to 350°F. Grease 8-inch square baking pan.

2 Melt butter and chocolate in medium saucepan over low heat. Remove from heat; stir in sugar. Beat in eggs and vanilla with wooden spoon. Stir together flour, baking powder and salt. Add to chocolate mixture, blending well. Stir in nuts. Pour batter into prepared pan.

3 Bake 30 to 35 minutes or until brownies begin to pull away from sides of pan. Cool completely in pan on wire rack. Frost with PEANUT BUTTER FROSTING, if desired. Cut into squares.

Peanut Butter Frosting

- 1 cup powdered sugar
- ¼ cup REESE'S® Creamy Peanut Butter
- 2 tablespoons milk
- ½ teaspoon vanilla extract

Combine all ingredients in small bowl; beat until smooth. If necessary add additional milk, ½ teaspoon at a time, until of desired consistency.

MAKES ABOUT ¾ CUP FROSTING

indulgent goodies

Chocolate Almond Macaroon Bars

MAKES ABOUT 24 TO 36 BARS

2 cups chocolate wafer cookie crumbs

6 tablespoons butter or margarine, melted

6 tablespoons powdered sugar

1 can (14 ounces) sweetened condensed milk (not evaporated milk)

3¾ cups MOUNDS® Sweetened Coconut Flakes

1 cup sliced almonds, toasted* (optional)

1 cup HERSHEY'S® SPECIAL DARK® Chocolate Chips or HERSHEY'S® Semi-Sweet Chocolate Chips

¼ cup whipping cream

½ cup HERSHEY'S® Premier White Chips

To toast almonds: Heat oven to 350°F. Spread almonds evenly on shallow baking sheet. Bake 5 to 8 minutes or until lightly browned.

1 Heat oven to 350°F. Grease 13×9×2-inch baking pan.

2 Combine crumbs, melted butter and powdered sugar in large bowl. Firmly press crumb mixture on bottom of prepared pan. Stir together sweetened condensed milk, coconut and almonds in large bowl, mixing well. Carefully drop mixture by spoonfuls over crust; spread evenly.

3 Bake 20 to 25 minutes or until coconut edges just begin to brown. Cool.

4 Place chocolate chips and whipping cream in medium microwave-safe bowl. Microwave at MEDIUM (50%) 1 minute; stir. If necessary, microwave at MEDIUM an additional 15 seconds at a time, stirring after each heating, until chips are melted and mixture is smooth when stirred. Cool until slightly thickened; spread over cooled bars. Sprinkle top with white chips. Cover; refrigerate several hours or until thoroughly chilled. Cut into bars. Refrigerate leftovers.

Peanut Butter and Milk Chocolate Chip Tassies

MAKES 3 DOZEN COOKIES

¾	cup (1½ sticks) butter, softened
1	package (3 ounces) cream cheese, softened
1½	cups all-purpose flour
¾	cup sugar, divided
1	egg, slightly beaten
2	tablespoons butter or margarine, melted
¼	teaspoon lemon juice
¼	teaspoon vanilla extract
1	cup HERSHEY'S® Milk Chocolate Chips
1	cup REESE'S® Peanut Butter Chips
2	teaspoons shortening (do not use butter, margarine, spread or oil)

1 Beat ¾ cup butter and cream cheese in medium bowl; add flour and ¼ cup sugar, beating until well blended. Cover; refrigerate about one hour or until dough is firm. Shape dough into 1-inch balls; press balls onto bottoms and up sides of about 36 small muffin cups (1¾ inches in diameter).

2 Heat oven to 350°F. Combine egg, remaining ½ cup sugar, melted butter, lemon juice and vanilla in small bowl; stir until smooth. Stir together milk chocolate chips and peanut butter chips. Set aside ⅓ cup chip mixture; add remaining chips to egg mixture. Evenly fill muffin cups with egg mixture.

3 Bake 20 to 25 minutes or until filling is set and lightly browned. Cool completely; remove from pan to wire rack.

4 Combine remaining ⅓ cup chip mixture and shortening in small microwave-safe bowl. Microwave at MEDIUM (50%) 30 seconds; stir. If necessary, microwave additional 10 seconds at a time, stirring after each heating, until chips are melted and mixture is smooth when stirred. Drizzle over tops of tassies.

Layered Cookie Bars

MAKES ABOUT 36 BARS

¾ cup (1½ sticks) butter or margarine

1¾ cups vanilla wafer crumbs (about 50 wafers, crushed)

6 tablespoons HERSHEY'S® Cocoa

¼ cup sugar

1 can (14 ounces) sweetened condensed milk (not evaporated milk)

1 cup HERSHEY'S® SPECIAL DARK® Chocolate Chips or HERSHEY'S® Semi-Sweet Chocolate Chips

¾ cup HEATH® BITS 'O BRICKLE® Toffee Bits

1 cup chopped walnuts

1 Heat oven to 350°F. Melt butter in 13×9×2-inch baking pan in oven. Combine crumbs, cocoa and sugar; sprinkle over butter.

2 Pour sweetened condensed milk evenly on top of crumbs. Top with chocolate chips and toffee bits, then nuts; press down firmly.

3 Bake 25 to 30 minutes or until lightly browned. Cool completely in pan on wire rack. Chill, if desired. Cut into bars. Store covered at room temperature.

Chippy Chewy Bars

MAKES ABOUT 48 BARS

- ½ cup (1 stick) butter or margarine
- 1½ cups graham cracker crumbs
- 1⅔ cups (10-ounce package) REESE'S® Peanut Butter Chips
- 1½ cups MOUNDS® Sweetened Coconut Flakes
- 1 can (14 ounces) sweetened condensed milk (not evaporated milk)
- ½ cup HERSHEY'S® SPECIAL DARK® Chocolate Chips, HERSHEY'S® Semi-Sweet Chocolate Chips or HERSHEY'S® Mini Chips Semi-Sweet Chocolate
- ¾ teaspoon shortening (do *not* use butter, margarine, spread or oil)

1 Heat oven to 350°F. Place butter in 13×9×2-inch baking pan. Heat in oven until melted; remove pan from oven. Sprinkle graham cracker crumbs evenly over butter; press down with fork.

2 Sprinkle peanut butter chips over crumbs; sprinkle coconut over chips. Drizzle sweetened condensed milk evenly over top.

3 Bake 20 minutes or until lightly browned.

4 Place chocolate chips and shortening in small microwave-safe bowl. Microwave at MEDIUM (50%) 30 seconds; stir. If necessary, microwave at MEDIUM an additional 10 seconds at a time, stirring after each heating, just until chips are melted when stirred. Drizzle evenly over top of baked mixture. Cool completely. Cut into bars.

White Chip Lemon Streusel Bars

MAKES 24 TO 36 BARS

1	can (14 ounces) sweetened condensed milk (not evaporated milk)
½	cup lemon juice
1	teaspoon freshly grated lemon peel
2	cups (12-ounce package) HERSHEY'S® Premier White Chips, divided
⅔	cup butter or margarine, softened
1	cup packed light brown sugar
1½	cups all-purpose flour
1½	cups regular rolled or quick-cooking oats
¾	cup toasted pecan pieces*
1	teaspoon baking powder
½	teaspoon salt
1	egg
½	teaspoon shortening

To toast pecans: Heat oven to 350°F. Spread pecans in thin layer in shallow baking pan. Bake, stirring occasionally, 7 to 8 minutes or until golden brown; cool.

1 Heat oven to 350°F. Lightly grease 13×9×2-inch baking pan. Combine sweetened condensed milk, lemon juice and lemon peel in medium bowl; set aside. Measure out ¼ cup and ⅓ cup white chips; set aside. Add remaining white chips to lemon mixture.

2 Beat butter and brown sugar with electric mixer on medium speed in large bowl until well blended. Stir together flour, oats, pecans, baking powder and salt; add to butter mixture, blending well. Set aside 1⅔ cups oats mixture. Add egg to remaining oats mixture, blending until crumbly; press onto bottom of prepared pan. Gently spoon lemon mixture on top, spreading evenly. Add reserved ⅓ cup white chips to reserved oats mixture. Sprinkle over lemon layer, pressing down lightly.

3 Bake 20 to 25 minutes or until lightly browned. Cool in pan on wire rack. Place remaining ¼ cup white chips and shortening in small microwave-safe bowl. Microwave at MEDIUM (50%) 30 seconds or until chips are melted and mixture is smooth when stirred. Drizzle over baked bars. Allow drizzle to set; cut into bars.

Peanut Butter Fudge Brownie Bars

MAKES 24 TO 36 BARS

1	cup (2 sticks) butter or margarine, melted
1½	cups sugar
2	eggs
1	teaspoon vanilla extract
1¼	cups all-purpose flour
⅔	cup HERSHEY'S® Cocoa
¼	cup milk
1¼	cups chopped pecans or walnuts, divided
½	cup (1 stick) butter or margarine
1⅔	cups (10-ounce package) REESE'S® Peanut Butter Chips
1	can (14 ounces) sweetened condensed milk (not evaporated milk)
¼	cup HERSHEY'S® SPECIAL DARK® Chocolate Chips or HERSHEY'S® Semi-Sweet Chocolate Chips

1 Heat oven to 350°F. Grease 13×9×2-inch baking pan.

2 Beat melted butter, sugar, eggs and vanilla in large bowl with electric mixer on medium speed until well blended. Add flour, cocoa and milk; beat until blended. Stir in 1 cup nuts. Spread in prepared pan.

3 Bake 25 to 30 minutes or just until edges begin to pull away from sides of pan. Cool completely in pan on wire rack.

4 Melt ½ cup butter and peanut butter chips in medium saucepan over low heat, stirring constantly. Add sweetened condensed milk, stirring until smooth; pour over baked layer.

5 Place chocolate chips in small microwave-safe bowl. Microwave at MEDIUM (50%) 45 seconds or just until chips are melted when stirred. Drizzle bars with melted chocolate; sprinkle with remaining ¼ cup nuts. Refrigerate 1 hour or until firm. Cut into bars. Cover; refrigerate leftover bars.

Marbled Cheesecake Bars

MAKES 24 TO 36 BARS

CHOCOLATE CRUST (recipe follows)

3   packages (**8 ounces each**) cream cheese, softened

1   can (**14 ounces**) sweetened condensed milk (not evaporated milk)

3   eggs

2   teaspoons vanilla extract

4   sections (½ ounce each) HERSHEY'S® Unsweetened Chocolate Baking Bar, melted

1 Prepare CHOCOLATE CRUST. Heat oven to 300°F.

2 Beat cream cheese in large bowl until fluffy. Gradually add sweetened condensed milk, beating until smooth. Add eggs and vanilla; mix well.

3 Pour half of batter evenly over prepared crust. Stir melted chocolate into remaining batter; drop by spoonfuls over vanilla batter. With metal spatula or knife, swirl gently through batter to marble.

4 Bake 45 to 50 minutes or until set. Cool in pan on wire rack. Refrigerate several hours until chilled. Cut into bars. Cover; store leftover bars in refrigerator.

Chocolate Crust: Stir together 2 cups vanilla wafer crumbs (about 60 wafers, crushed), ⅓ cup HERSHEY'S® Cocoa and ½ cup powdered sugar. Stir in ½ cup (1 stick) melted butter or margarine until well blended. Press mixture firmly onto bottom of ungreased 13×9×2-inch baking pan.

Peanut Butter Polka Dot Bars

¾	cup butter or margarine, softened
¾	cup REESE'S® Creamy Peanut Butter
2	cups light brown sugar, packed
2	eggs
1	teaspoon vanilla extract
2½	cups quick-cooking rolled oats
2½	cups all-purpose flour
1	teaspoon baking soda
½	teaspoon salt
	CHOCOLATE FILLING (recipe follows)
1⅓	cups (10-ounce package) REESE'S® MINI PIECES Candies

1 Heat oven to 350°F. Beat butter, peanut butter and brown sugar until well blended. Add eggs and vanilla; beat thoroughly.

2 Stir together oats, flour, baking soda and salt; gradually add to butter mixture. (Dough will be thick.) Remove 2 cups dough; set aside. Press remaining dough onto bottom of 13×9×2-inch baking pan.

3 Prepare CHOCOLATE FILLING. Spread filling evenly over dough. Sprinkle candy pieces evenly over filling. Crumble reserved dough evenly over filling.

4 Bake 25 minutes or until top is golden brown. (Chocolate will be soft.) Cool completely in pan on wire rack; cut into bars.

Chocolate Filling: Melt ½ cup (1 stick) butter or margarine in saucepan over low heat. Stir in ⅔ cup HERSHEY'S® Cocoa and ⅓ cup sugar. Add 1 can (14 ounces) sweetened condensed milk; cook, stirring constantly, until smooth and thick. Remove from heat; stir in 1½ teaspoons vanilla extract.

cupcakes & mini cakes

Mini Brownie Cups

MAKES 24 BROWNIES

¼ cup (½ stick) light margarine

2 egg whites

1 egg

¾ cup sugar

⅔ cup all-purpose flour

⅓ cup HERSHEY'S® Cocoa

½ teaspoon baking powder

¼ teaspoon salt

MOCHA GLAZE (recipe follows)

1 Heat oven to 350°F. Line small muffin cups (1¾ inches in diameter) with paper bake cups or spray with vegetable cooking spray.

2 Melt margarine in small saucepan over low heat; cool slightly. Beat egg whites and egg in small bowl with electric mixer on medium speed until foamy; gradually add sugar, beating until slightly thickened and light in color. Stir together flour, cocoa, baking powder and salt; gradually add to egg mixture, beating until blended. Gradually add melted margarine, beating just until blended. Fill muffin cups ⅔ full with batter.

3 Bake 15 to 18 minutes or until wooden pick inserted in center comes out clean. Remove from pan to wire rack. Cool completely. Prepare MOCHA GLAZE; drizzle over tops of brownie cups. Let stand until glaze is set. Store, covered, at room temperature.

Mocha Glaze

¼ cup powdered sugar

¾ teaspoon HERSHEY'S® Cocoa

¼ teaspoon powdered instant coffee

2 teaspoons hot water

¼ teaspoon vanilla extract

Stir together powdered sugar and cocoa in small bowl. Dissolve instant coffee in water; gradually add to sugar mixture, stirring until well blended. Stir in vanilla.

1st Birthday Cupcakes

MAKES ABOUT 2½ DOZEN CUPCAKES

- 1⅔ cups all-purpose flour
- 1½ cups sugar
- ½ cup HERSHEY'S® Cocoa
- 1½ teaspoons baking soda
- 1 teaspoon salt
- ½ teaspoon baking powder
- 2 eggs
- ½ cup shortening
- 1½ cups buttermilk or sour milk*
- 1 teaspoon vanilla extract
- ONE-BOWL BUTTERCREAM FROSTING (recipe follows)

*To sour milk: Use 4½ teaspoons white vinegar plus milk to equal 1½ cups.

1 Heat oven to 350°F. Line muffin cups (2½ inches in diameter) with paper bake cups.

2 Stir together flour, sugar, cocoa, baking soda, salt and baking powder in large bowl. Add eggs, shortening, buttermilk and vanilla. Beat on low speed of mixer 1 minute, scraping bowl constantly. Beat on high speed 3 minutes, scraping bowl occasionally. Fill muffin cups ½ full with batter.

3 Bake 18 to 20 minutes or until wooden pick inserted in center comes out clean. Remove from pan to wire rack. Cool completely. Frost with ONE-BOWL BUTTERCREAM FROSTING.

HERSHEY'S® Chocolate Cake:

Heat oven to 350°F. Grease two 9-inch round baking pans; line bottoms with wax paper. Prepare batter as directed above; pour into prepared pans. Bake 30 to 35 minutes or until wooden pick inserted in center comes out clean. Cool 10 minutes; remove from pans to wire racks. Remove paper. Cool completely. Frost with ONE-BOWL BUTTERCREAM FROSTING.

One-Bowl Buttercream Frosting

- 6 tablespoons butter or margarine, softened
- 2⅔ cups powdered sugar
- ½ cup HERSHEY'S® Cocoa
- ⅓ cup milk
- 1 teaspoon vanilla extract

Beat butter in medium bowl. Add powdered sugar and cocoa alternately with milk and vanilla, beating to spreading consistency (additional milk may be needed).

MAKES ABOUT 2 CUPS FROSTING

Espresso Filled Mini Cakes

MAKES ABOUT 14 MINI CAKES

2	cups sugar
1¾	cups all-purpose flour
¾	cup HERSHEY'S® Cocoa
1½	teaspoons baking powder
1½	teaspoons baking soda
1	teaspoon salt
2	eggs
1	cup milk
½	cup vegetable oil
2	teaspoons vanilla extract
1	cup boiling water

ESPRESSO CREAM FILLING (recipe follows) or apricot preserves or other flavor of your choice

COCOA GLAZE (recipe follows)

1 Heat oven to 350°F. Grease and lightly flour fourteen 6-ounce custard cups.

2 Stir together sugar, flour, cocoa, baking powder, baking soda and salt in large bowl. Add eggs, milk, oil and vanilla; beat on medium speed of mixer 2 minutes. Stir in water (batter will be thin). Fill each prepared cup with scant ½ cup batter. Place custard cups on cookie sheet.

3 Bake 20 to 25 minutes or until wooden pick inserted in center comes out clean. Cool 5 minutes on wire racks; remove mini cakes from cups. Cool completely. Cut mini cakes horizontally about 1 inch from top. Spread bottom with ESPRESSO CREAM FILLING or preserves; replace top of cake. Drizzle with COCOA GLAZE. Refrigerate until serving time. Refrigerate leftover cakes.

ESPRESSO CREAM FILLING:
Combine 1 cup (½ pint) cold whipping cream, ¼ cup powdered sugar and 2 teaspoons powdered instant espresso (or powdered instant coffee) in small bowl; beat until stiff. Makes about 2 cups filling.

Cupcakes: Line muffin pan (2½ inches in diameter) with paper bake cups. Fill ½ full with batter. Bake at 350°F 20 minutes or until wooden pick inserted in center comes out clean. Fill and glaze as directed in recipe. Makes about 3 dozen cupcakes.

Cocoa Glaze

½	**cup whipping cream**
1½	**teaspoons light corn syrup**
½	**cup HERSHEY'S® Cocoa**
½	**cup sugar**
1	**tablespoon butter**
1½	**teaspoons vanilla extract**

Stir together whipping cream and corn syrup in small saucepan. Stir together cocoa and sugar in small bowl; add to cream mixture, stirring well. Add butter. Cook over low heat, stirring constantly, until butter melts and mixture is smooth. Do not boil. Remove from heat; stir in vanilla. Cool to desired consistency.

MAKES ABOUT 1 CUP GLAZE

Note: Glaze may be stored in airtight container in refrigerator up to 2 weeks. Reheat over low heat, Stirring constantly.

Glazed Cranberry Mini-Cakes

MAKES ABOUT 3 DOZEN MINI-CAKES

⅓ cup butter or margarine, softened

⅓ cup granulated sugar

⅓ cup packed light brown sugar

1 egg

1¼ teaspoons vanilla extract

1⅓ cups all-purpose flour

¾ teaspoon baking powder

¼ teaspoon baking soda

¼ teaspoon salt

2 tablespoons milk

1¼ cups coarsely chopped fresh cranberries

½ cup coarsely chopped walnuts

1⅔ cups HERSHEY'S® Premier White Chips, divided

WHITE GLAZE (recipe follows)

1 Heat oven to 350°F. Lightly grease or paper-line 36 small muffin cups (1¾ inches in diameter).

2 Beat butter, granulated sugar, brown sugar, egg and vanilla in large bowl until fluffy. Stir together flour, baking powder, baking soda and salt; gradually blend into butter mixture. Add milk; stir until blended. Stir in cranberries, walnuts and ⅔ cup white chips (reserve remaining chips for glaze). Fill muffin cups almost full with batter.

3 Bake 18 to 20 minutes or until wooden pick inserted in center comes out clean. Cool 5 minutes; remove from pans to wire rack. Cool completely. Prepare WHITE GLAZE; drizzle over top of mini-cakes. Refrigerate 10 minutes to set glaze.

White Glaze: Place remaining 1 cup HERSHEY'S® Premier White Chips in small microwave-safe bowl; sprinkle 2 tablespoons vegetable oil over chips. Microwave at MEDIUM (50%) 30 seconds; stir. If necessary, microwave at MEDIUM an additional 30 seconds or just until chips are melted when stirred.

Molten Chocolate-Cherry Cakes

MAKES 6 SERVINGS

CHOCOLATE DIPPED CHERRIES (recipe follows)

⅔ cup plus 1 tablespoon sugar, divided

¾ cup (1½ sticks) butter or margarine

½ cup HERSHEY'S® Cocoa

¼ cup whipping cream

1½ teaspoons vanilla extract

¼ cup all-purpose flour

2 eggs

2 egg yolks

⅓ cup maraschino cherries, finely chopped

Sweetened whipped cream (optional)

1 Prepare CHOCOLATE DIPPED CHERRIES.

2 Heat oven to 400°F. Grease six ¾-cup soufflé dishes or six 6-ounce custard cups. Sprinkle insides evenly with 1 tablespoon sugar. Place dishes in 13×9×2-inch baking pan or a jelly-roll pan.

3 Melt butter in medium saucepan. Remove from heat. Whisk in cocoa, ⅓ cup sugar, whipping cream and vanilla. Whisk in flour just until combined. Set aside.

4 Beat eggs, egg yolks and remaining ⅓ cup sugar in large bowl with electric mixer on high speed about 5 minutes or until slightly thickened and lemon-colored. Beat in chocolate mixture on medium speed. Pour about ¼ cup into each prepared custard cup. Sprinkle chopped cherries evenly over each. Carefully pour remaining chocolate mixture into each cup.

5 Bake 13 to 15 minutes or just until top of each cake looks dry. Do not overbake. Let stand in cups 3 minutes. Loosen sides of each. Invert onto serving plates. Serve warm topped with whipped cream and a CHOCOLATE DIPPED CHERRY.

Chocolate Dipped Cherries:

Drain 6 maraschino cherries with stems. Pat dry with paper towels. Place ¼ cup HERSHEY'S® SPECIAL DARK® Chocolate Chips or HERSHEY'S® Semi-Sweet Chocolate Chips and ½ teaspoon shortening (do not use butter, margarine, spread or oil) in small microwave-safe bowl. Microwave at MEDIUM (50%) for 45 seconds. Stir until chips are melted. Dip cherries into chocolate mixture. Place on wax paper-lined tray. Refrigerate until serving time.

Tip: For make-ahead convenience, prepare the cakes but do not bake. Cover with plastic wrap and refrigerate for up to 3 hours. Let stand at room temperature 30 minutes, then bake as directed.

P.B. Chips Brownie Cups

MAKES 1½ DOZEN BROWNIE CUPS

- **1** cup (2 sticks) butter or margarine
- **2** cups sugar
- **2** teaspoons vanilla extract
- **4** eggs
- **¾** cup HERSHEY'S® Cocoa or HERSHEY'S® SPECIAL DARK® Cocoa
- **1¾** cups all-purpose flour
- **½** teaspoon baking powder
- **½** teaspoon salt
- **1⅔** cups (10-ounce package) REESE'S® Peanut Butter Chips, divided

1 Heat oven to 350°F. Line 18 muffin cups (2½ inches in diameter) with paper or foil bake cups.

2 Place butter in large microwave-safe bowl. Microwave at MEDIUM (50%) 1 to 1½ minutes or until melted. Stir in sugar and vanilla. Add eggs; beat well. Add cocoa; beat until well blended. Add flour, baking powder and salt; beat well. Stir in 1⅓ cups peanut butter chips. Divide batter evenly into muffin cups.

3 Bake 25 to 30 minutes or until surface is firm. Immediately sprinkle remaining ⅓ cup peanut butter chips over muffin tops, pressing in slightly. Cool completely in pan on wire rack.

Filled Rich Chocolate Cupcakes

FILLING (recipe follows)

3	cups all-purpose flour
2	cups sugar
⅔	cup HERSHEY'S® Cocoa
2	teaspoons baking soda
1	teaspoon salt
2	cups water
⅔	cup vegetable oil
2	tablespoons white vinegar
2	teaspoons vanilla extract

1 Prepare FILLING; set aside. Heat oven to 350°F. Line muffin cups (2½ inches in diameter) with paper bake cups.

2 Stir together flour, sugar, cocoa, baking soda and salt in large bowl. Add water, oil, vinegar and vanilla; beat on medium speed of mixer 3 minutes. Fill muffin cups ⅔ full with batter. Spoon 1 level tablespoon FILLING into center of each cupcake.

3 Bake 20 to 25 minutes or until wooden pick inserted in cake portion comes out clean. Remove to wire rack. Cool completely.

Filling

1	package (8 ounces) cream cheese, softened
⅓	cup sugar
1	egg
⅛	teaspoon salt
1	cup HERSHEY'S® SPECIAL DARK® Chocolate Chips, HERSHEY'S® Semi-Sweet Chocolate Chips or HERSHEY'S® Mini Chips Semi-Sweet Chocolate

Beat cream cheese, sugar, egg and salt in small bowl; beat until smooth and creamy. Stir in chocolate chips.

Goblin's Delight Filling: Add 2 teaspoons grated orange peel, 4 drops yellow food color and 3 drops red food color to FILLING before stirring in chips.

Valentine Filling: Stir 4 to 5 drops red food color into FILLING.

Peanut Butter Chip Filling: Omit chocolate; stir in 1 cup REESE'S® Peanut Butter Chips.

Mini Cocoa Cupcake Kabobs

MAKES ABOUT 4 DOZEN CUPCAKES

- 1 cup sugar
- 1 cup all-purpose flour
- ⅓ cup HERSHEY'S® Cocoa
- ¾ teaspoon baking powder
- ¾ teaspoon baking soda
- ½ teaspoon salt
- 1 egg
- ½ cup milk
- ¼ cup vegetable oil
- 1 teaspoon vanilla extract
- ½ cup boiling water
- LICKETY-SPLIT COCOA FROSTING (recipe follows)
- Jelly beans or sugar nonpareils and/or decorating frosting
- Marshmallows
- Strawberries
- Wooden or metal skewers

1 Heat oven to 350°F. Spray small muffin cups (1¾ inches in diameter) with vegetable cooking spray.

2 Stir together sugar, flour, cocoa, baking powder, baking soda and salt in medium bowl. Add egg, milk, oil and vanilla; beat on medium speed of mixer 2 minutes. Stir in boiling water (batter will be thin). Fill muffin cups about ⅔ full with batter.

3 Bake 10 minutes or until wooden pick inserted in center comes out clean. Cool slightly; remove from pans to wire racks. Cool completely. Frost with LICKETY-SPLIT COCOA FROSTING. Garnish with jelly beans, nonpareils and/or frosting piped onto cupcake. Alternate cupcakes, marshmallows and strawberries on skewers.

Lickety-Split Cocoa Frosting:

Beat 3 tablespoons softened butter or margarine in small bowl until creamy. Add 1¼ cups powdered sugar, ¼ cup HERSHEY'S® Cocoa, 2 to 3 tablespoons milk and ½ teaspoon vanilla extract until smooth and of desired consistency. Makes about 1 cup frosting.

Note: Number of kabobs will be determined by length of skewer used and number of cupcakes, marshmallows and strawberries placed on each skewer.

Toffee Topped Pineapple Upside-Down Cakes

MAKES 4 (4-INCH) CAKES

¼	cup light corn syrup
¼	cup (½ stick) butter or margarine, melted
1	cup HEATH® BITS 'O BRICKLE® Toffee Bits
4	pineapple rings
4	maraschino cherries
¼	cup (½ stick) butter or margarine, softened
⅔	cup sugar
1	egg
1	tablespoon rum or 1 teaspoon rum extract
1⅓	cups all-purpose flour
2	teaspoons baking powder
⅔	cup milk

1 Heat oven to 350°F. Lightly coat inside of 4 individual 2-cup baking dishes with vegetable oil spray.

2 Stir together 1 tablespoon corn syrup and 1 tablespoon melted butter in each of 4 baking dishes. Sprinkle each with ¼ cup toffee. Center pineapple rings on toffee and place cherries in centers.

3 Beat softened butter and sugar in small bowl until blended. Add egg and rum, beating well. Stir together flour and baking powder; add alternately with milk to butter-sugar mixture, beating until smooth. Spoon about ¾ cup batter into each prepared dish.

4 Bake 25 to 30 minutes or until wooden pick inserted in center comes out clean. Immediately invert onto serving dishes; cool slightly before serving. Refrigerate leftovers.

party time treats

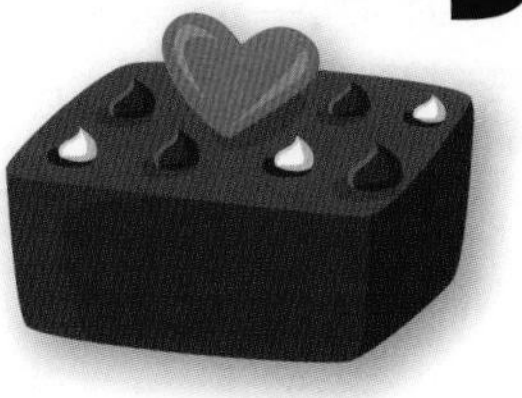

Holiday Red Raspberry Chocolate Bars

MAKES 24 TO 36 BARS

2½   cups all-purpose flour

1   cup sugar

¾   cup finely chopped pecans

1   egg, beaten

1   cup (2 sticks) cold butter or margarine

1   jar (12 ounces) seedless red raspberry jam

1⅔   cups HERSHEY'S® Milk Chocolate Chips, HERSHEY'S® SPECIAL DARK® Chocolate Chips, HERSHEY'S® Semi-Sweet Chocolate Chips or HERSHEY'S® MINI KISSES®BRAND Milk Chocolates

1 Heat oven to 350°F. Grease 13×9×2-inch baking pan.

2 Stir together flour, sugar, pecans and egg in large bowl. Cut in butter with pastry blender or fork until mixture resembles coarse crumbs; set aside 1½ cups crumb mixture. Press remaining crumb mixture on bottom of prepared pan. Stir jam to soften; carefully spread over crumb mixture in pan. Sprinkle with chocolate chips. Crumble reserved crumb mixture evenly over top.

3 Bake 40 to 45 minutes or until lightly browned. Cool completely in pan on wire rack; cut into bars.

Midnight Chocolate Cheesecake Cookie Cups

MAKES 30 DESSERT CUPS

¼ cup (½ stick) butter, softened

¼ cup shortening

½ cup sugar

1 egg

½ teaspoon vanilla extract

1 cup all-purpose flour

2 tablespoons HERSHEY'S® SPECIAL DARK® Cocoa or HERSHEY'S® Cocoa

½ teaspoon baking powder

⅛ teaspoon salt

CHOCOLATE FILLING (recipe follows)

Whipped topping or sweetened whipped cream

30 HERSHEY'S® KISSES®BRAND SPECIAL DARK® Mildly Sweet Chocolates, unwrapped

1 Heat oven to 350°F. Paper or foil line 30 small (1¾-inch diameter) muffin cups.

2 Beat butter and shortening in medium bowl until fluffy. Beat in sugar, egg and vanilla. Stir together flour, cocoa, baking powder and salt. Gradually blend into butter mixture, blending well.

3 Drop rounded teaspoonful of dough into each prepared muffin cup. Using back of spoon, push dough up sides of muffin cup forming crater in cup. (If you have difficulty with this step, refrigerate pans for about 10 minutes and then continue.) Prepare CHOCOLATE FILLING; evenly divide into muffin cups. (Cups will be very full.)

4 Bake 15 minutes or until cheesecake is set. Cool completely in pan on wire rack. Cover; refrigerate until ready to serve. To serve, top each cheesecake with whipped topping rosette and chocolate piece.

Chocolate Filling: Beat 2 packages (3 ounces each) softened cream cheese and ¼ cup sugar until well blended. Beat in 1 egg, 1 teaspoon vanilla extract and ⅛ teaspoon salt. Place 12 unwrapped HERSHEY'S® KISSES®BRAND SPECIAL DARK® Mildly Sweet Chocolates in small microwave-safe bowl. Microwave at MEDIUM (50%) 15 seconds at a time, stirring after each heating, until chocolates are melted and smooth when stirred. Cool slightly, blend into cheesecake batter.

Peanut Butter Cup Rocky Road Squares

MAKES ABOUT 20 SERVINGS

38	to 40 REESE'S® Peanut Butter Cups Miniatures
1	cup (2 sticks) butter or margarine
1¼	cups HERSHEY'S® Cocoa, divided
2	cups sugar
4	eggs
2½	teaspoons vanilla extract, divided
1¾	cups all-purpose flour
1	can (14 ounces) sweetened condensed milk (not evaporated milk)
1	jar (7 ounces) marshmallow crème
½	cup coarsely chopped peanuts

1 Heat oven to 350°F. Line 13×9×2-inch baking pan with foil, extending foil beyond sides. Grease foil. Remove wrappers from peanut butter cups. Cut each peanut butter cup into 4 pieces; set aside.

2 Place butter in large microwave-safe bowl. Microwave at MEDIUM (50%) 1 minute or until butter is melted. Stir in ¾ cup cocoa until smooth. Add sugar, 3 eggs and 1 teaspoon vanilla; blend well. Blend in flour; spread in prepared pan. Bake 15 minutes.

3 Meanwhile, combine sweetened condensed milk, remaining ½ cup cocoa, remaining egg and remaining 1½ teaspoons vanilla. Pour over baked layer. Return to oven; bake 20 to 25 minutes or until set.

4 Place marshmallow crème by heaping teaspoonfuls over hot surface. Allow to soften about 5 minutes; carefully spread over surface. Immediately sprinkle peanut butter cup pieces and peanuts over marshmallow. Cool completely in pan on wire rack. Refrigerate until thoroughly chilled.

5 Lift dessert from pan using foil as handles; place on cutting board. Cut into squares. To serve, gently heat in microwave at MEDIUM about 10 seconds or 200°F oven until marshmallow softens. (Dessert may also be allowed to soften at room temperature until ready to serve.) Cover; refrigerate leftovers.

Brownie Petit Fours

MAKES ABOUT 3 DOZEN PETIT FOURS

½	cup (1 stick) butter or margarine, melted
1	cup sugar
1	teaspoon vanilla extract
2	eggs
½	cup all-purpose flour
⅓	cup HERSHEY'S® Cocoa
¼	teaspoon baking powder
¼	teaspoon salt
½	cup chopped walnuts (optional)
2	cups (12-ounce package) HERSHEY'S® Mini Chips Semi-Sweet Chocolate
3	tablespoons shortening (do not use butter, margarine, spread or oil)
	Sprinkles or decorator's icing (optional)

1 Heat oven to 350°F. Line 9-inch square baking pan with foil; grease foil.

2 Stir together butter, sugar and vanilla in bowl. Add eggs; beat well with spoon. Stir together flour, cocoa, baking powder and salt; gradually add to egg mixture, beating until well blended. Stir in walnuts, if desired. Spread batter evenly in prepared pan.

3 Bake 20 to 25 minutes or until brownie begins to pull away from sides of pan. Cool completely in pan on wire rack; refrigerate about 2 hours.

4 Using edges of foil, lift brownie out of pan. Peel off foil; cut into 1¼ inch-squares and allow to warm up to room temperature.

5 Line tray with wax paper. Melt small chocolate chips and shortening in small heavy saucepan over very low heat. Dip each brownie square into melted chocolate, covering completely. (Return to heat if chocolate cools and is hard to coat.) Gently tap on side of pan to allow extra chocolate to drip off. Place on prepared tray. Allow chocolate to set at room temperature or refrigerate until set (about 30 minutes); decorate as desired. (Sprinkles should be added just before chocolate sets.)

Patriotic Cocoa Cupcakes

2	cups sugar
1¾	cups all-purpose flour
¾	cup HERSHEY'S® Cocoa
2	teaspoons baking soda
1	teaspoon baking powder
1	teaspoon salt
2	eggs
1	cup buttermilk or sour milk*
1	cup boiling water
½	cup vegetable oil
1	teaspoon vanilla extract
	VANILLA FROSTING (recipe follows)
	Chocolate stars or blue and red decorating icings (in tubes)

*To sour milk: Use 1 tablespoon white vinegar plus milk to equal 1 cup.

1 Heat oven to 350°F. Grease and flour muffin cups (2½ inches in diameter) or line with paper bake cups.

2 Combine dry ingredients in large bowl. Add eggs, buttermilk, water, oil and vanilla; beat on medium speed of mixer 2 minutes (batter will be thin). Fill cups ⅔ full with batter.

3 Bake 15 minutes or until wooden pick inserted in center comes out clean. Remove cupcakes from pan. Cool completely. To make chocolate stars for garnish, if desired, cut several cupcakes into ½-inch slices; cut out star shapes from cake slices. Frost remaining cupcakes. Garnish with chocolate stars or with blue and red decorating icings.

Vanilla Frosting: Beat ¼ cup (½ stick) softened butter, ¼ cup shortening and 2 teaspoons vanilla extract in large bowl. Add 1 cup powdered sugar; beat until creamy. Add 3 cups powdered sugar alternately with 3 to 4 tablespoons milk, beating to spreading consistency. Makes about 2⅓ cups frosting

Witch's Hat Chocolate Cupcakes

MAKES ABOUT 2½ DOZEN CUPCAKES

- ¾ cup (1½ sticks) butter or margarine, softened
- 1⅔ cups sugar
- 3 eggs
- 1 teaspoon vanilla extract
- 2 cups all-purpose flour
- ⅔ cup HERSHEY'S® Cocoa
- 1¼ teaspoons baking soda
- 1 teaspoon salt
- ¼ teaspoon baking powder
- 1⅓ cups water
- ORANGE CREAM FILLING (recipe follows)

1 Heat oven to 350°F. Line muffin cups (2½ inches in diameter) with paper bake cups.

2 Combine butter, sugar, eggs and vanilla in large bowl; beat on medium speed of mixer 3 minutes. Stir together flour, cocoa, baking soda, salt and baking powder; add alternately with water to butter mixture, beating after each addition until just blended. Fill muffin cups ⅔ full with batter.

3 Bake 20 to 25 minutes or until wooden pick inserted in center comes out clean. Remove from pans to wire racks. Cool completely.

4 Prepare ORANGE CREAM FILLING. Cut 1½-inch cone-shaped piece from center of each cupcake; reserve. Fill each cavity with scant tablespoon prepared filling. Place reserved cake pieces on filling, pointed side up. Refrigerate before serving. Cover; refrigerate leftover filled cupcakes.

Orange Cream Filling

- ½ cup (1 stick) butter or margarine, softened
- 1 cup marshmallow crème
- 1¼ cups powdered sugar
- ½ to 1 teaspoon freshly grated orange peel
- ½ teaspoon vanilla extract
- 2 to 3 teaspoons orange juice
- Red and yellow food colors (optional)

Beat butter in small bowl until creamy; gradually beat in marshmallow crème. Gradually add powdered sugar, orange peel and vanilla, beating until blended. Add orange juice and food colors, if desired; beat until smooth and of desired consistency.

MAKES ABOUT 1⅓ CUPS FILLING

Sweetheart Layer Bars

MAKES 24 TO 36 BARS

1	**cup (2 sticks) butter or margarine, divided**
1½	**cups finely crushed unsalted thin pretzels or pretzel sticks**
1	**cup HERSHEY'S® MINI KISSES®BRAND Milk Chocolates**
1	**can (14 ounces) sweetened condensed milk (not evaporated milk)**
¾	**cup HERSHEY'S® Cocoa**
2	**cups MOUNDS® Sweetened Coconut Flakes, tinted***

*To tint coconut: Place 1 teaspoon water and ½ teaspoon red food color in small bowl; stir in 2 cups coconut flakes. With fork, toss until evenly coated.

1 Heat oven to 350°F.

2 Place ¾ cup butter (1½ sticks) in 13×9×2-inch baking pan; place in oven just until butter melts. Remove from oven. Stir in crushed pretzels; press evenly onto bottom of pan. Sprinkle chocolates over pretzel layer.

3 Place sweetened condensed milk, cocoa and remaining ¼ cup butter (½ stick) in small microwave-safe bowl.

Microwave at MEDIUM (50%) 1 to 1½ minutes or until mixture is melted and smooth when stirred; carefully pour over chocolate layer in pan. Top with coconut; press firmly down onto chocolate layer.

4 Bake 25 to 30 minutes or until lightly browned around edges. Cool completely in pan on wire rack. Cut into heart-shaped pieces with cookie cutters or cut into bars.

Touchdown Brownie Cups

MAKES ABOUT 17 CUPCAKES

- **1** cup (2 sticks) butter or margarine
- **½** cup HERSHEY'S® Cocoa or HERSHEY'S® SPECIAL DARK® Cocoa
- **1** cup packed light brown sugar
- **½** cup granulated sugar
- **3** eggs
- **1** teaspoon vanilla extract
- **1** cup all-purpose flour
- **1⅓** cups chopped pecans, divided

1 Heat oven to 350°F. Line 2½-inch muffin cups with foil or paper bake cups.

2 Place butter in large microwave-safe bowl; cover. Microwave at MEDIUM (50%) 1½ minutes or until melted. Add cocoa; stir until smooth. Add brown sugar and granulated sugar; stir until well blended. Add eggs and vanilla; beat well.

Add flour and 1 cup pecans; stir until well blended. Fill prepared muffin cups about ¾ full of batter; sprinkle about 1 teaspoon remaining pecans over top of each.

3 Bake 20 to 25 minutes or until tops begin to dry and crack. Cool completely in cups on wire rack.

Jack-O-Lantern Brownie

- ¾ cup (1½ sticks) butter or margarine, melted
- 1½ cups sugar
- 1½ teaspoons vanilla extract
- 3 eggs
- ¾ cup all-purpose flour
- ½ cup HERSHEY'S® Cocoa
- ½ teaspoon baking powder
- ¼ teaspoon salt
- Yellow and red food color
- 1 can (16 ounces) vanilla frosting

Suggested garnishes: HERSHEY'S® MINI KISSES®BRAND Milk Chocolates, assorted candies as TWIZZLERS® NIBS® Licorice Bits, TWIZZLERS® PULL-N-PEEL®, HEATH® English Toffee Bits

1 Heat oven to 350°F. Grease 12-inch round pizza pan. If using a disposable pan, place on baking sheet to bake.

2 Beat melted butter, sugar and vanilla with spoon in large bowl. Beat in eggs. Stir in dry ingredients; beat with spoon until well blended. Spread in pan.

3 Bake 20 to 22 minutes or until top springs back when touched lightly in center. Cool completely. Add yellow and red food color to frosting for desired shade of orange. Frost brownie; garnish to resemble a jack-o-lantern.

Hanukkah Dreidel Brownies

MAKES ABOUT 3 DOZEN BROWNIES

1	cup (2 sticks) butter or margarine, softened
2	cups sugar
2	teaspoons vanilla extract
4	eggs
¾	cup HERSHEY'S® Cocoa or HERSHEY'S® SPECIAL DARK® Cocoa
1	cup all-purpose flour
½	teaspoon baking powder
¼	teaspoon salt
2	cups (12-ounce package) HERSHEY'S® Premier White Chips, divided
1	tablespoon shortening (not butter, margarine, spread or oil)
1	tube (4.25 ounce) royal blue decorating icing (optional)

1 Heat oven to 350°F. Line 13×9×2-inch baking pan completely with foil, leaving extra on sides for handles.

2 Place butter in large microwave-safe bowl. Microwave at HIGH (100%) 2 to 2½ minutes or until melted. Stir in sugar and vanilla. Add eggs, one at a time, beating well with spoon after each addition. Add cocoa; beat until well blended. Add flour, baking powder and salt; beat well. Pour batter into prepared pan.

3 Bake 30 to 35 minutes or just until brownies begin to pull away from sides of pan. Cool completely in pan on wire rack. Invert brownie onto serving tray; peel off foil.

4 Shape into dreidel: About 3 inches from bottom of each long side, cut triangular pieces to bottom center, forming point of dreidel. Cut about 1 inch from top edge; cut in half and attach 1 piece as handle.

5 Place 1 cup white chips and shortening in small microwave-safe bowl. Microwave at MEDIUM 1 minute; stir until mixture is melted and smooth when stirred. Spread on dreidel, about 1 inch from top and 2 sides, forming 7-inch square. Decorate with remaining white chips and decorating icing, if desired. Cut into bars.

index

Brownies in a Jar *(page 8)*

INDEX

Peanut Butter Cup Rocky Road
Squares *(page 54)*

Mini Cakes

Cupcakes

1st Birthday Cupcakes *(page 36)*

Chocolate Almond Macaroon
Bars *(page 23)*

Treats

Midnight Chocolate Cheesecake
Cookie Cups *(page 52)*